BEG
AQUARIUM

By Mervin F. Roberts

(t.f.h.)

Distributed in the U.S. by T.F.H. Publications, Inc., 211 West Sylvania Avenue, PO Box 427, Neptune, NJ 07753; in England by T.F.H. (Gt. Britain) Ltd., 13 Nutley Lane, Reigate, Surrey; in Canada to the pet trade by Rolf C. Hagen Ltd., 3225 Sartelon Street, Montreal 382, Quebec; in Canada to the book trade by H & L Pet Supplies, Inc., 27 Kingston Crescent, Kitchener, Ontario N28 2T6; in Southeast Asia by Y.W. Ong, 9 Lorong 36 Geylang, Singapore 14; in Australia and the South Pacific by Pet Imports Pty. Ltd., P.O. Box 149, Brookvale 2100, N.S.W. Australia; in South Africa by Valid Agencies, P.O. Box 51901, Randburg 2125 South Africa. Published by T.F.H. Publications, Inc., Ltd.

INTRODUCTION

This is a book about preparing an aquarium to house your fishes. Necessarily it must commence with a consideration of what kind and how many fishes you plan to start with.

One rule of thumb is that you can house one inch of fish, exclusive of the tail, per gallon of water without aeration or filtration. The inch of fish rule is based on fishes of average proportions and activity.

A full-grown platy by this rule might measure one inch from the mouth to the base of the tail and ten such fish in a ten-gallon tank is a safe top figure to start with.

If you aerate your tank you can increase the number of fishes by 100 per cent; the same ten-gallon tank might accommodate up to twenty "inches of fish" by using a pump and airstone.

Finally, by using a filtering device, you can increase the "inches of fish" to three inches per gallon.

Because of their bright colors and the ease with which they can be bred, platies are an excellent choice for the beginning aquarist. The fish shown here are gold "Mickey Mouse" platies, the name "Mickey Mouse" denoting the black markings at the base of the tail.

Zebra danios make a fascinating addition to the community aquarium, for they school closely together and are always on the move. They are extremely hardy fish that can even endure relatively cool temperatures with no ill effects, as long as the temperature change is not sudden. Photo by H. J. Richter.

Your choice of fishes is limited by their disposition and your wallet. For instance, if you want twenty inches of fish you can install them in an aerated ten-gallon aquarium, or a "still water twenty." If your budget is limited to ten dollars, for the twenty "fish-inches," you still can do very nicely with something like this for instance:

fish			fish inches
2	neon tetras	=	2
2	small angels	=	4
2	zebra fish	=	2
3	red platies	=	3
2	black mollies	=	3
2	catfish	=	3
2	barbs	=	3
15			20

If you choose less placid fishes you should give them more room. Your pet dealer will gladly brief you on this point; better yet, you can obtain an inexpensive illustrated beginner's guide at any pet shop carrying a complete line of pet supplies and have the fun of picking out the fishes yourself.

If you choose some of the labyrinth fishes, also called the "bubble nesters," like the pearl, kissing or three spot gouramis, the paradise fish or the Siamese fighting fish, you might increase somewhat the number of inches of fish per gallon, but by and large, the formula is a good one and it should not be treated lightly.

THE AQUARIUM

➪ Your choice of the number of fishes may dictate the size of tank. Possibly, however, you already bought your tank to fit in a particular spot in a room or on a table where the dimensions of the space limit the dimensions of the tank.

Aquaria are available in nearly every shape you might want, and you can have any special size, within reason, made to order. Before you buy, however, you should consider these two factors:

1. The tank with the greatest surface area per gallon will support the greatest number of fishes per gallon. Low, wide tanks of this design are often called breeding tanks.

2. The tank with the greatest front window area will provide you with the best view of your pets. Tanks like this are often called "community" or "show" tanks. It is strongly recommended that the beginner's first tank be a community-show tank.

If you feel that you cannot afford a pump and airstone or filter right away, you should get the show tank anyway and follow the inch-per-gallon formula. Later, when your wallet permits, you can round out the setup with the additional equipment and add more fish if you desire.

One of the most colorful platy varieties is the red tuxedo platy. These fish, along with swordtails, mollies and guppies, bear living young. Birth of a brood of these livebearers is an exciting event for the novice aquarist.

Rummy-nose tetras appear quite often in tropical fish shops. Their colorful looks and peaceful temperament make them an asset to a community aquarium. Photo by Dr. D. Terver, Nancy Aquarium, France.

Tanks are constructed of drawn glass or polished plate glass. Drawn glass is popular for tanks of less than 20 gallons and polished plate is more often found in the larger sizes—say over fifty gallons. Sections of drawn glass which are relatively flawless can be selected, but in larger aquaria where clear glass in thicker sections is required, the choice is generally polished plate. Today some glass manufacturers produce a product they called "demi-plate" or "semi-plate". This is high quality drawn glass in thicker sections than ordinary drawn window glass. The best thing for a potential buyer to do is to simply insist on a new tank made by a reputable manufacturer. Leave the manufacturer's label on the aquarium if it's on the outside so you will know who made it when or if something should go wrong for the first few days after it has been filled.

The plastic frame should be fairly thick and the butt-jointed glass edges evenly joined. Today's all-glass plastic-framed aquaria will not rust and need maintenance. The tank should have a cover. The cover can be a sheet of glass with the edges sanded or ground down or, better still, a plastic or stainless steel hood housing a light. You will probably want to light your tank in the evenings anyway, and an

5

attractive hood containing one or several incandescent or fluorescent tubes is a fine way to keep the fishes in, dust and cigarette ashes out and provide a mounting and reflector for the lights. Today many tankmakers have inexpensive reflectors that match their tanks and fit perfectly. Another advantage of the reflector top is that the heat of the light is directed into the water where it aids in keeping the aquarium temperature at the proper level. This is advantageous, because you will use more light during the long winter nights and less during long summer days.

If you don't want a reflector, then by all means get a sheet of glass cut about an inch larger than the tank dimensions and clip off the rear corners to permit access for the heater and filter connections. The edges of the glass can be sanded or filed smooth with ordinary emery paper, a slowly rotating wet grindstone or a fine cut file. Don't worry about cutting off the air with the tank top; you would have to seal the edges with aquarium cement in order to deprive the fish of oxygen.

HEATERS

▷ Unless the aquarium is to be kept in a temperate room where it never gets colder than 72°F, you will need a heater. Many different kinds of aqaurium heaters have been designed. Heated water has been sprayed into tanks and drained off, hot water pipes have been run through tanks, aquarium water has been circulated through a heated vessel, electric light bulbs have been immersed directly in the water or immediately above it and, of course, aquarium heaters electrically energized and thermostatically controlled have been designed and manufactured especially for you, the aquarist.

Of all the things strongly advised that the aquarist not "gadget" with, the thermostatic heater unit heads the list. Buy a new high quality heater from your pet dealer, and spend the time you saved by not trying to make one enjoying your charges instead of risking electrocution. Most aquarium heaters are mounted in a glass tube along with the thermostat.

Heaters are rated in watts. The heater rating should correspond to the tank size and the maximum temperature difference between the approximately 74°F you will want and the coldest you expect the room will become.

To find the heater watt-rating you need, you should figure ¼ watt per gallon per degree Fahrenheit difference.

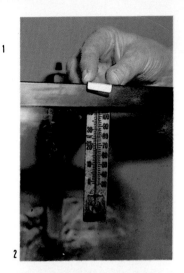

(1) Short plants that won't conceal heaters should be placed at the front. (2) A thermometer is an inexpensive but necessary accessory.

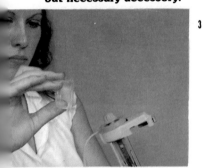

(3) Protective cover for heater. (4) Mounting heater in rear corner. (5) Rotation of the heater control knob can raise or lower water temperature. (6) Tall plants can conceal heater and filter tubes. Photos by Glen S. Axelrod.

Most readily available small tetras are hardy and are compatible in a community aquarium. Seen here are neon tetras (with red stripe), a black neon (uppermost fish) and a pair of black tetras (with roundish body and black vertical bars).

For a ten-gallon tank that you want to keep at 77° F , in a room that may cool to 57° F at night, the formula will work out:

¼ (factor) times 10 (gallons) times 77 minus 57 (degrees difference) comes to ¼ x 10 x 20 = 50 watts.

Another easy formula to remember, under normal house conditions, is 5 watts per gallon of water. The tank shape and the type of top are contributing factors.

Since there is a remote but ever-present risk of a thermostat sticking closed and leaving the heater on, you should not over-invest in heater wattage. If your estimate falls between two available size heaters, choose the smaller one. Regardless of the size of the heater, the electric consumption will be about the same since the thermostat control will promptly turn off any heater when the temperature you want is reached.

If the temperature in the tank falls five degrees at night and returns to 77°F by noon daily, you need not worry. It's cool in the tropics too, at night.

The exact location of the heater in the tank should suit your taste since currents set up by the heated water, the swimming fish and the airstone or filter will heat the tank throughout anyway.

THE THERMOSTAT

▷ The thermostat, which is usually mounted in the same tube as the heater, is essentially a temperature operated electric switch. You set the temperature by adjusting a screw or racking a knob, and when the temperature rises to the pre-determined setting, the current to the heater is cut off and it remains off until the temperature falls a degree or so, enough in any event to turn the current to the heater back on. A good thermostat will operate for years with absolutely no attention.

To adjust your thermostat you simply immerse the unit in a vessel of tap water and plug it into an electrical outlet after you have checked the water with a thermometer and found it to have the exact temperature you desire for your fish. A good place to do this is right in the aquarium (before you put in your fish).

With the temperature at what you want it to be, you adjust the thermostat so that the pilot light just blinks at the slightest change in adjustment. It should take a half-hour to stabilize the temperature in the thermostat before making this adjustment. If you become confused, ask your pet dealer to set it for you. Modern well-designed thermostats are practically foolproof and are easily adjusted.

Years ago a common complaint about thermostats was that they caused radio interference. Today any thermostat worth its salt is equipped with a built-in condenser across the line which effectively eliminates static. Some thermostats are also equipped with fuses. However, if your home is properly fused this added refinement is not essential. Whenever purchasing any electrical equipment, look for the manufacturer's guarantee!

THE THERMOMETER

▷ A thermometer is a "must". Obviously it will not keep the fish warm, but it will reassure you that the heater is functioning properly. The range you care about is from 40 to 110°F. Don't buy one that goes up to 212°F where water boils or down to 32° where it freezes. These extremes are of no interest to the aquarist and only mean that in the range he is interested in figures are compressed and difficult to read. Thermometers are made to float, stand on the bottom, stick to the outside of the tank or hang into the aquarium. Any one is all right—take your pick.

(1-4) Riser tubes and charcoal chambers should be attached to the undergravel filter plates before the plates are placed.

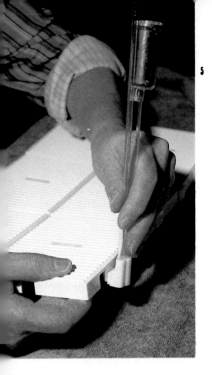

(5) Modular undergravel filters can fit a variety of tank shapes. (6) Undergravel filter plates should cover the entire aquarium bottom. (7) Power filters hang on the outside of the tank; they provide efficient filtration. Photos by Glen S. Axelrod.

GRAVEL

Aquarium gravel serves several purposes:

It anchors plants.

It can add color to the tank.

It acts as a catchall for fine debris which might otherwise always be stirred up by the fish or the air.

It harbors bacteria that degrade minute particles of food that the fish miss as well as other organic debris.

Your choice of gravel should be guided by the following factors:

1. The color should be pleasing to your eye.

2. The particle sizes should make for an open texture (open enough to allow water to circulate through it).

3. The edges of the particles should not be cutting sharp. Avoid crushed glass for gravel no matter how pretty it is. If you have a smooth chunk of glass of a color you like, by all means use it, but use it as a stone and do not crush it into gravel.

4. The gravel should be chemically inert. Gravel taken from the seashore should not be used. Shells in water tend to make it alkaline and later you may decide that your fish are better suited to neutral or acid waters. Some artificially dyed sands are not

One or two corydoras catfish should be added to the community aquarium. They help keep the aquarium clean by using their barbels to dig bits of uneaten food out of the gravel. Photo by H. J. Richter.

Some barbs (such as tiger barbs) tend to nip at the fins of other fishes, but cherry barbs (shown here) don't usually bother other fishes. The male is the redder fish. Photo by R. Zukal.

perfectly colorfast and unless you purchase them from an aquarium dealer who has had personal experience with that particular batch of material, do not use it.

5. It should be sufficient in quantity to anchor the plants and not too much more. Two inches of gravel in back, banked down to three quarters of an inch in front is more than ample for any twenty gallon tank. If an undergravel filter is used the gravel should be three inches deep at the back of the tank and two inches at the front. Larger tanks will accommodate bigger plants with bigger root systems, so you might find it well to increase the depth a bit only in the back corners.

6. The gravel should be clean. No soil need be added to feed the plants. They will get what they need from the wastes the fish give off. If the plants seem to need more food, there are several inexpensive non-fouling mineral foods for aquarium plants you can buy in your pet shop.

The color and texture of the gravel can be enhanced, if you like, by scattering a few chips of crushed garnet, petrified wood or some rounded white quartz pebbles on the top. Avoid crevices and debris traps where uneaten food or a dead fish might decay out of sight.

Gravel being poured (1) and smoothed over undergravel filter plates (2). The bases of decorations such as driftwood should be buried under the gravel (3 and 4).

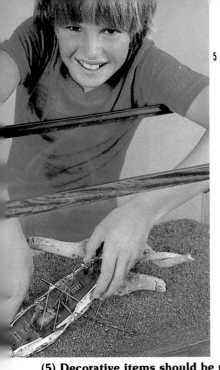

(5) Decorative items should be placed into tank before plants are added. (6) Attaching tubing to undergravel filter stem. (7 and 8) Placing plastic plants into the tank. Photos by Glen S. Axelrod.

To calculate the amount of gravel you need, you can assume an average depth of one inch. If your ten-gallon tank has a base measuring 10″ x 20″ or 200 square inches and you want an average depth of one inch, then 200 x 1 or 200 cubic inches of gravel will be required. Now, one pound of gravel occupies about seventeen cubic inches; so, 200 divided by 17 equals about 12 pounds of gravel required for a ten-gallon tank. Since it is generally put up in five pound packages, you might do well to take fifteen pounds and save the surplus for sloping the gravel. A rule of thumb is 1½ pounds of gravel per gallon aquarium capacity.

No matter how well washed your gravel is supposed to be, you should wash it yourself before you use it. The simplest way is to pour gravel into a plastic bucket (that has never been used for detergent or any other chemical) to a depth of four or five inches, and flush it well with a garden hose. Impatience with this detail might lead to regrets later on.

Male Siamese fighting fish (bettas) battle with one another constantly, but a single male may be kept in a community tank with little or no danger to the other fishes. Photo by H. J. Richter.

Angelfish are very hardy and will thrive well in a community tank. The long filamentous fins, however, make them easy prey for fin-nippers. As they mature they become less mild-mannered and may themselves become fin-nippers. Photo by Gene Wolfsheimer.

SETTING UP THE AQUARIUM

➡ Wash the tank with clear, slightly warm (not hot) water. Don't use soap, detergents or mineral spirits.

The best tank made will probably leak if it is lifted or moved with water in it. Avoid placing the tank on radiator covers, near open windows or drafty areas or where it is accessible to pets and small children. When you move your tank, move it empty and carry it by holding the bottom near the corners. Try to choose a location near an electrical outlet and, if possible, have a drawer, shelf or cabinet nearby for the few simple accessories you will surely want.

After placing the tank, you may put in the washed gravel. If an undergravel filter is going to be used, it should be placed in the tank before adding the gravel. The tank may be half filled with water and then planted. It is easier to work out the landscaping if the leaves are allowed to float up naturally as planting proceeds. Don't make the mistake of filling the aquarium up to the brim before you plant; your hands will make the water overflow.

17

Placing a tight-fitting cover (1) and light fixture (2). (3) A background scene for placement on the back of the tank. (4) Attaching airline to vibrator pump. Photos by Glen S. Axelrod.

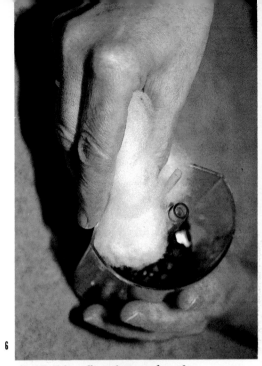

(5) Hand breaks water's fall into tank. (6) Filter floss being placed atop charcoal in box filter. (7) Concealing a box filter among plants. (8) Aquarium scraper. Photos by Glen S. Axelrod.

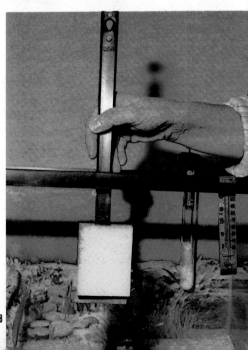

(1) A completed aquarium ready to receive fishes. (2) Fishes should be floated in their plastic bags for a while to allow the temperature of the water in the bag to slowly equalize with that of the aquarium. Photos by Judy Ronay.

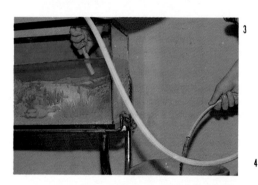

(3) Siphoning water from the tank. (4 and 5) Single-edge razor blade being used to remove caked deposits. (6) Checking for deposits on heater tube. Photos by Glen S. Axelrod.

Mollies are always a favorite of beginning aquarists. They are available in solid black or marbled patterns.

"SETTING UP"

☞ Place your tank on a flat level support. The load should be distributed all around the plastic tank frame, not on the center of the glass.

If you want to color the outside of the back glass, you can purchase an inexpensive lacquer for this job in your pet shop. It will neatly mask your outside filter or other distracting sights.

When you clean your tank you may want to sterilize it with salt. Rinse it with a warm brine solution, or take a clean rag covered with salt crystals and rub over all the inside surfaces. To make brine, mix a pound of aquarium salt into a pot of warm (not hot) tap water and swish it around the tank for a while. Then pour off the liquid and rinse out the tank before putting it in place to be filled with fresh tap water.

If the gravel is from a source which you suspect might be contaminated or otherwise unclean, it can be sterilized by pouring boiling water over it and then rinsing it cool with tap water *before putting it into the tank.* If the boiling water releases any noticeable odor or color, you should trace and eliminate the trouble or go elsewhere for your gravel.

Your plants should be well washed in tepid, gently running water. Be gentle with roots and leaves, but use plenty of water and go over the plants carefully for bugs, including grub-like cutworms and scorpion-like dragonfly larvae. The former eat vegetation and the latter will kill your fish.

With a clean tank, washed gravel, an inside box filter or an undergravel filter, if that is what you plan to use, water, a few rocks if you like and the previously cleaned plants, you are ready to start setting up. Put the packed box filter in the rear corner or the undergravel filter flat on the tank bottom. Pour the damp gravel into the tank and push it around so that it is deep where you plan to put most of the larger rooted plants. Most people generally plant heavily in the back and side areas. This is only natural, but if you have any other ideas there is nothing but your own good taste to tell you where to plant.

Place no mud or earth or humus or fertilizer under the gravel. Use just plain clean gravel—period. The plants will not starve if you have fish in the tank.

Blood red swordtails (below) and tuxedo swordtails (opposite) are hardy, peaceful fishes that are recommended for the beginner's aquarium.

Arrange any rocks you plan to use. A large chunk of quartz, granite, petrified wood, agate or similar inert rock is often an attractive detail on the bottom. Some aquarium ornaments are manufactured especially for this purpose. Be careful, however, to avoid anything which might tip over and break a glass side.

You can place the damp sand in the tank, sloping it as you wish, and then lay a plate or bowl on the bottom and pour in the cool water slowly. The plate prevents the gravel from being stirred up. Now the plants can be added to the tank.

Finally, fill the tank to within a half inch of the top and mount the heater and plug it in. Put a thermometer in the water. Set on the reflector and/or the glass cover. The only openings in the top should be for the heater and the filter.

FILTRATION AND AERATION

To keep the greatest number of fishes in the clearest water under the conditions most conducive to good health you should use a filter. A filter performs several functions:

1. It circulates the water and eliminates hot or cold zones.
2. It aerates water by bringing it to the surface and by passing a stream of air through it.
3. It filters out tiny particles of dirt, debris and plant life which would otherwise cloud the aquarium.

By this combined action of filtering, circulating and aerating, you can safely double the number of fish in the tank and, with a minimum of attention, keep the water crystal clear.

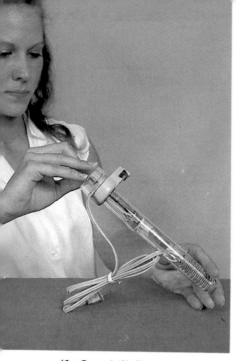

(1, 2 and 3) Periodic checking and maintenance of the heater, which can be taken apart. (4) Dirt accumulated in airline blocks airflow from the pump. Photos by Glen S. Axelrod.

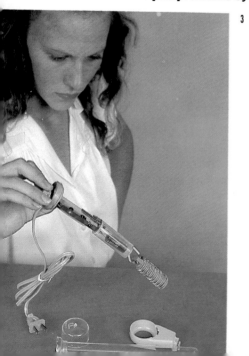

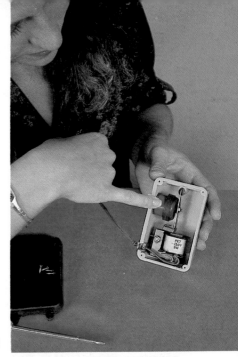

(5) Removal of the bottom of this vibrator pump allows access to diaphragm (6). (7) Removing the air chamber to unbolt vibrator arm from diaphragm (8) for replacement. Photos by Glen S. Axelrod.

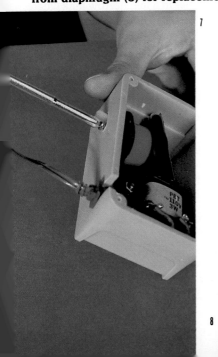

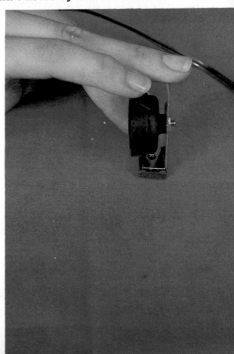

A small school of cardinal tetras will add a bit of flashy color to the aquarium. Photo by H. J. Richter.

Another important thing to remember about a filter is that it permits you to keep a good number of fishes in a tall, narrow tank where you can enjoy the view. Such a tank without aeration or filtration could support relatively few fishes.

One thing a filter cannot do is remove all the debris or uneaten food which settles to the bottom of your tank. For this you need a siphon or a dip tube.

A filter system can be reasonably quiet. If it is noisy it is suspect. The aquarist can assure himself of quiet, trouble-free operation by observing this simple rule.

Have the pet dealer demonstrate the pump and filter system he proposes to sell you. A hum no louder than the hum of an electric refrigerator should be expected, but if the pump chugs loudly or chatters, don't buy it. If it "throws" oil don't buy it.

Today we have many excellent efficient, clean operating, quiet pumps on the market. They require practically no maintenance and they will remain relatively quiet for years of trouble-free service.

The valves in the airline are precision instruments and if treated with reasonable care they will last forever. The tube connection nearest the knurled knob is the exit and should be connected to the filter or airstone tube. The tube entering or passing through the bottom of the valve is connected to the pump. If the valve has two tube connections at the bottom and one a half inch higher you can run air into either bottom tube and tap off a controlled rate of flow to a filter or airstone through the upper tube, the remaining air passing out the other bottom tube to additional filters or airstones, if you desire.

To test a valve before you use it, simply blow through the lower tube and (plugging the other bottom tube if present) slowly turn open the knurled knob a turn or two. The air should flow quietly and evenly as you manipulate the valve. If the valve stem turns too easily or too stiffly to adjust readily, the bonnet (over the valve body) can be screwed down a fraction of a turn with pliers. Do not tighten the bonnet unless the valve is partly open or you will break the needle or damage the valve seat.

Most valves are furnished with brass mounting plates and if you have several accessories you may buy a bank of three to five valves mounted on a convenient plastic plate which is designed to hang over the edge of the aquarium.

Pumps are classified into two main groups: vibrator or piston. The piston types are usually longer lasting, are much more expensive

Serpae tetras are also schooling fish and are commonly available in pet shops. They are peaceful and hardy. Photo by R. Zukal.

The harlequin rasbora is a colorful schooling fish that is a welcome addition to a community tank of small fishes. Photo by H. J. Richter.

and can handle a greater load. Vibrator types are cheaper but sometimes noisier. Select the best pump you can afford. In the piston types take care of exposed belts and pulleys if you have small children or animals about the house. Some of the better piston pumps have sealed units, protecting childrens' fingers from harm. Buy a good pump; the higher initial investment is well worth the difference.

FILTERS

There are several basic types of filters. The beginner should choose either the inside box filter, an undergravel filter or an outside power filter. Each is efficient and each has advantages.

The outside power filter takes up no room in the tank. It can be mounted on the back of the tank and if the tank's rear window is painted or covered with a decoration, you cannot see the device. Only the inlet and outlet tubes will show, and these can be hidden among the plants.

An inexpensive and popular filter is the inside box filter. It can be partially buried in the gravel in a rear corner of the tank; the only thing entering the aquarium is one thin air tube. This filter sends up a stream of air bubbles which carry the filtered water up with them. This filter is, in itself, a vigorous aerator and is designed to prevent small fish from swimming into it. If you use an inside box filter you certainly do not need an airstone, too. If you choose an outside power filter be sure the intake siphon has a screen or similar device on it to keep small fish out.

The outside power filter will aerate the water if the return tube is aimed so as to direct the clean water across the surface. Airstones are sometimes used in conjunction with outside power filters.

The tank should be full up to within one half inch of the moulding. If it is low the filtering efficiency of an outside power filter will be impaired and possibly noisy. Of course, an inside box filter will not be affected by a slight change in the depth of the water.

A popular development in aquarium filtration is the undergravel filter. Its purpose is to pull debris and ammonia into the sand where the bacteria can break it down into useful byproducts. These types of filters can be utilized with a regular inside box filter, or other types of filters. They are very successful and they keep the tank meticulously clean. Plants seem to grow exceptionally well when these filters are used, and they have the added convenience of not being visible.

With all filters, stick to name brands. There are many poorly made filters on the market which are easily broken. Rely upon your petshop dealer to guide you in the selection of the best type filter for your use.

Many aquarists and fish breeders use airstones exclusively. Owners of "community" show tanks feel that the added advantage of a filter is important. Certainly more fish can thrive in a filtered aquarium than in one that is only aerated. The author has observed that deep, narrow, crowded community show tanks are generally equipped with filters while low, wide, shallow breeding tanks are merely aerated. The beginning aquarist will surely start with a community show tank, and to get the most from it a filter and an airstone should be used. The flow of bubbles is, in itself, an attraction.

THE NET

A net seems to be such a simple thing to make right, yet the market is flooded with attractive but useless plant leaf breakers and patience destroyers.

The overall length should be several inches longer than the depth of the tank. This will help you to keep your hands dry, but more important it will make for easy manipulation.

Pet shops sell plant nutrient solutions or nutrient plugs that allow many species of plants to be grown in a newly established aquarium. An assortment of plants such as this will give most aquarium fishes a feeling of security, thus promoting good color, good growth and, in some cases, spawning behavior. Photo by A. van den Nieuwenhuizen.

The sides and the end should form right angles. If they do not, you will have trouble taking a fish out of a corner, especially if it is near the bottom.

The handle should be fairly stiff but still springy and thin enough to permit rapid maneuvering in the tank. Most fish are caught up against the glass and the slight spring permits the handle to be bent during this maneuver.

The mesh on most good nets today is nylon or a similar synthetic fabric, and although somewhat stiffer than cotton it will give years of service without rotting out. The mesh should be fine enough to keep fins and scales from getting hooked, yet open enough so you can sweep it through the water without much resistance.

The net should pocket the fish deeply enough so you can gently grasp the quarry with the cloth around it when making a transfer. Shallow nets and fish on the floor are closely associated. The pocket should not taper sharply or the fish may become jammed if he swims directly into it.

The width of the net should be about one-third the minimum dimension of the tank. A second net of smaller size is very useful for baby fish, and it also helps when you want to drive stubborn fish into the larger net.

PLANTS

Pick the plants that appeal to you. If the plants you pick out have roots, then bury the roots in the gravel. Do it gently. Avoid burying the crown (this is the point where the leaves or stems begin).

If the plants you buy do not have roots but are merely bunched with a bit of lead wire or a rubber band at the cut end, you can unwrap them and plant the cut ends or just let them float; some will eventually root themselves.

Don't spend too much money on too many plants in the beginning. Follow the advice of your dealer. If the water and light are right, then what you have will prosper and grow, and if the conditions are wrong for a particular kind of plant, chances are good that you can find something else which will grow like a weed. You might hedge a bit by getting several varieties.

You can use leafy plants to good advantage to mask the heater and filter. Large plants, with large leaves, are the best plants for a community-show aquarium.

Special planting tongs are available for adjusting and trimming plants once the aquarium has been established.

Large swordplants make excellent aquarium centerpieces. They require plenty of strong overhead light and a sufficient amount of gravel in which to anchor their roots. Photo by R. Zukal.

White Cloud Mountain fish are readily available, inexpensive and extremely hardy. They are also one of the easy-to-breed egglayers.

THE SIPHON

A siphon is invaluable. It is a must. It will cost you pennies and no aquarist should be without one. The tube should be a soft flexible rubber or plastic hose about five feet long and three-eighths or one-half inch in diameter. On one end fasten a rigid plastic tube a couple of inches longer than the tank depth. The plastic tube should be smaller in inside diameter than the rubber hose. In that way, anything which clears the plastic will not clog the hose. The siphon will be necessary in conjunction with the dip tube. Neither supplants the other. Use the dip tube to clean up a little debris or uneaten food. Use the siphon to draw off larger quantities of water and sediment periodically.

THE SCRAPER

The scraper is a simple tool consisting of a long handle and a replaceable razor blade in a holder. It is as good a way as any to clean the algae from the tank window. Many aquarists suspect their water is cloudy, only to discover crystal water and a thin film of brown or green algae on the window.

Dip tube, siphon, scraper, net—these accessories are only infrequently used, but to have the right tool when you need it will help make aquarium management as much fun as it is easy.

With the heater going and the thermostat adjusted, the lights working, or sunlight streaming in a few hours a day on the plants and the filter bubbling quietly, wait a day or so and then go to your pet dealer for your fish.

You are off to a good start—enjoy yourself!